Outback Bushfire Miracle Recovery

RICHARD HARVEY AM

2019
Adelaide

Copyright © Richard Harvey AM
Copyright © of photographs held by individual photographers where indicated. All other images copyright © Richard Harvey AM
All rights reserved. Except for any fair dealing permitted under the Copyright Act, no part of this book may be reproduced by any means without prior permission. Inquiries should be made to the publisher.

National Library of Australia Cataloguing-in-Publication entry
Creator: Richard Harvey AM
Title: Outback Bushfire Miricle Recovery
ISBN: 9781921816727 Soft cover
       9781921816734 Hard cover
       9781921816741 Epub
       9781921816758 PDF

Making a lasting impact

An imprint of the ATF Publishing Group
ATF (Australia) Ltd
PO Box 504 Hindmarsh
SA 5007
ABN 90 116 359 963
www.atfpress.com

Cover Photograph: Bruce Moulds
Graphic Design & Layout: Trevor Hill

Layout by: Lane Print & Post, Adelaide - www.laneprint.com.au
Paper: 150gsm Satin Art
Font: Body Font; Times New Roman 12pt
Title & Heading Fonts; Baskerville Bold & Times New Roman

Outback Bushfire Miracle Recovery

By

Richard Gilbert Mungo Harvey AM

2019
Adelaide

I dedicate this book to the doctors and nurses at the Intensive Care and Burns Unit at the Royal Adelaide Hospital.

They saved my life.

Richard Harvey 1985.

Acknowledgements

My writing is done in long hand, largely unintelligible to anyone but myself, because of the damage to my hands, caused by the fire.

It was therefore necessary to have it typed. Alex Reynolds, my nurse, has a great friend Leia Homer. She came after work or on the weekends and typed the first version.

Alex and I looked at it and decided it needed expanding because I had set out the facts, period. It lacked any sort of description or emotion. "The cat sat on the mat. It was a black cat". This was how it was written with very little personal expression of the horror of what had happened and how I fought to get my life back. Alex helped to alter this to a much better version.

Finally, Shylie Mackintosh, my daughter, typed the last draft. To these three people I owe the final version of the "Miracle". I am very grateful to them all, thank you.

Foreword

It is not often that we are privileged to read a first-hand account from a patient who has suffered life-threatening burns and survived.

In the recounting of his saga, Richard Harvey has taken us inside his world of being a patient, an aspect that those of us looking in and helping on the outside, seldom see.

Richard Harvey reports the calculation of the likelihood of 'crude mortality' from such a serious burn, and shows that he had, in fact, suffered a potentially mortal injury.

The primary factors defeating the results of this addition were Richard's physical toughness and his powerful mental resolve, assisted by the support of his loved ones and many friends.

From a treatment perspective there were a few key actions that aided this positive outcome.

Firstly, the early institution of intravenous fluid resuscitation and oxygen from his local doctor, played a vital role in minimising ongoing tissue damage.

Then his rapid transfer to the State Burns Unit provided access to the centre best able to manage his injury.

Thirdly, resuscitation continued with more intravenous fluid (several buckets-full in fact) which helped to normalise his physiology. He then underwent endotracheal intubation to preserve his deteriorating airway (produced by swelling within his airways as a result of heat and smoke inhalation).

While life-saving, this unfortunately rendered him temporarily unable to speak, and thus unable to communicate with his loved ones.

Fifthly, he then began a long period of Intensive Care Management, where his vital functions were micro-managed by their excellent team.

Following his admission, several of us from the Burns Unit had a conference as a result of which we decided to embark on the treatment considered at that time to be the regimen that would give Richard the best chance of survival, that of early and aggressive burn wound excision.

Risky in itself, this excision would remove those chemicals produced by the burn that can produce critical lung injury and lead to multi-organ failure.

Unfortunately, at that time this meant that Richard would be subjected to multiple skin grafting procedures, necessitating a long stay in hospital.

Now, as a result of research and development at this same Burns Unit, techniques of manufacturing a composite skin replacement may mean that multiple skin grafts are a thing of the past.

Those who are mentioned most frequently in this book are those who provided Richard with daily human interaction and care, and by supporting and cajoling, by changing dressings and feeding, the Specialist Burn Nurse provides the care, without which the scientific plan does not succeed.

During and after the acute wound healing phase is complete, Physiotherapy and Occupational Therapy begin the long task of rehabilitation, without which return to life outside the Burns Unit, is even more difficult.

Richard has typically made light of how his life has irrevocably changed as a result of this terrible injury, but has not mentioned all the things that he could once do but no longer can – for example, playing a deadly game of tennis.

Those who are lucky enough to meet him socially from time to time, are still pleased to say: "It's good to have you back Richard."

Dr Ian Leitch
Head of Burns Unit
Royal Adelaide Hospital 1990's

Contents

		Page
Chapter 1	*The fire day*	9
Chapter 2	*Family background*	17
Chapter 3	*Life after university*	21
Chapter 4	*Onto Yalkuri*	27
Chapter 5	*Daughter-in-law recount*	37
Chapter 6	*The RAH*	39
	The staff	43
Chapter 7	*First stage of recovery*	45
	Second stage of recovery	47
Chapter 8	*Visitors*	49
	Diet	51
	Clothing	52
	Last days in the burns unit	53
Chapter 9	*Kiandra Hospital*	55
Chapter 10	*Going home*	59
Chapter 11	*Life after burns*	63
Chapter 12	*So, what happens now?*	67

Chapter 1

The Fire

It was a pleasant spring day, with a north breeze in the morning at Yalkuri, on November the 12th, 1990. Yalkuri is a mixed farming property on the south west corner of the Narrung Peninsula in South Australia, near the mouth of the Murray River.

Our stockman, Brendan Savage, was doing a routine check of livestock, which involved cleaning the water troughs from which the stock drank. He was in the middle of cleaning the trough in Avocet Paddock, when he noticed, to his consternation that a small fire had started under his motorbike. Dry grass seeds had lodged next to the exhaust pipe, which was hot. They fell to the ground and lit up the dry grass under the bike.

He quickly moved the bike out of danger, but had no means of putting out the fire. So, he jumped on his motorbike and raced off to find the station manager, me, whom he knew was inspecting some steers for sale.

We picked up my son David, the overseer, from the dairy, loaded up the fire truck, and went back to the fire scene.

By this time the fire had spread from the grass paddock into the adjoining scrub, an 800-acre area of Mallee scrub, untouched by man or fire for at least 80 years, probably much longer.

We were able to put out the grass fire in Avocet, but the scrub was another matter.

I alerted the local country fire service brigades at Meningie and Narrung, and we started to plough a fire break along the northern side of the scrub to protect our grass paddock.

The southern side of the scrub was the Coorong, the eastern and western sides had fire breaks that had been ploughed years before.

It was late afternoon by the time the fire units arrived, and they had commissioned a bulldozer to create a fire break in the scrub. By 1 a.m. the next morning, the wind had dropped, and the fire was contained so we all went to bed, very tired.

However, the next morning the wind direction changed from north to south west, and the scrub fire (being still alight) jumped the dozer break and proceeded north towards the northern firebreak.

Brendan Savage and I were spot burning patches of grass on this firebreak, with Bruce Moulds in attendance with our small fire truck.

The fire arrived at the break, but the strong wind caused sparks to jump the break in one place and start another grass fire. We tried to put this out, but failed, so went back to the nearest water tank some distance away, to fill up.

After a short time, I could see the fire approaching, so we retreated, Brendan on his bike, Bruce driving the truck, and me standing on the passenger side running board. We were nearly out of danger when the truck hit a large stone, and I fell off. By the time I stood up, the fire was upon me.

Now there are certain rules that we are taught to follow if we are caught in a fire. If it is a scrub fire, you try and run away as fast as you can. This is because a scrub fire is usually slower than a grass fire, but far more dangerous to life. A grass fire travels more quickly, but once it is past you, the burnt area is still extremely hot but at least it has finished burning. So, my best chance of survival was to run through the fire as quickly as possible, but imagine a wall of fire about your height in front of you. It is a horrible and ghastly sight.

But training prevailed so I ran towards the fire, and through it I went, falling on my hands and knees on the already burnt area. This was still red hot with embers, but I think at this point I was in severe shock, and everything became a bit of a blur.

Meanwhile, Bruce had realised I had fallen off and bravely drove through the fire to pick me up. He got through unscathed to the burnt area where I was on my hands and knees. He asked me how I was, but I must have been in shock because I did not reply. He picked me up, walked me to the truck and put me in the passenger seat with still no response from me.

He tried to start the truck, but the fire had vaporised the petrol in the fuel lines, so the truck would not start. There I sat, not really aware of anything that had happened, nor the desperate emotions of the man sitting next to me frantically trying to start the engine.

After what seemed like forever, but was more like five horrible minutes the truck did start, and we drove away.

It is hard to describe how I felt. I seemed to be conscious for a bit, feeling absolutely terrible and in great pain and would lapse into unconsciousness.

Meanwhile, my eldest son James (an accountant), was at a meeting in his firm's office in Adelaide. Half way through, he was handed a note to say that I had been burnt.

Apparently the Yalkuri fire had jumped the fire break, and was heading North, propelled by a stiff southerly breeze. He frantically hopped in his car, collected some clothes, and headed off on the Prince's Highway to Yalkuri. By the time he got to Mount Barker, he could see the smoke of the fire some 80km away.

The fire in the scrub paddock Kartoo, 1990, taken from Yalkuri Homestead.

He was able to then get in touch with Bruce Moulds, and they met in a paddock south of the Meningie Road. Between them, they transferred me to the car he was driving, sitting me up in the front seat. Now this is the first instance of a life-saving move, because if I had been lying down my airways could have blocked, and I would have died. I was barely conscious at this stage, but at times could just talk a little.

He then drove me to Bruce Mould's house, which was on the Meningie Road, and once at the house, called an ambulance which unfortunately for me, was out on another job.

James followed instructions from the ambulance service and hosed me down with water while I was still sitting in the car. He also had a 4-litre container of water which he put on my lap, and told me to splash it on my face and head.

Once again, I do not remember being hosed down. This was the second life-saving measure, as it helped to hydrate me and cool my skin down.

He describes my burnt skin – which was my face, hands, arms, upper body and part of one leg, as being white and thin-looking, not hanging in strips.

My upper body was so badly burnt because I had been wearing a synthetic shirt which melted on to my chest. Wearing synthetic clothing was a rule of fighting a fire that I had obviously not remembered.

My legs and hair were largely saved because I wore cotton moleskin trousers, woollen socks, leather boots, and I was wearing an Akubra hat.

So, we set off from Bruce's house, of which I can't remember anything, to the hospital at Meningie. Halfway there we were met by the ambulance coming out to get me.

James talked to the ambulance driver, and it was decided it would be quicker if he took me the rest of the way. This was given more impetuous by me saying from my seat "just get me there for Christ's sake!" By this time, I was beginning to feel real pain and was very uncomfortable, and very much awake. The drive seemed endless.

With the ambulance leading us we proceeded at an even faster pace, to the Meningie hospital. I think it took about one to one and a half hours from the time I fell in the fire until we finally reached the hospital. Had it been any longer, I would probably have died.

My local doctor, Brian Symon, happened to be on duty at the hospital and looked pretty shaken when he saw me. James remembers that Brian and a nurse started immediately to apply a thick cream to the burnt areas of my body. My life was still hanging by a thread.

Meanwhile, back at the scene, the fire continued to burn north, across the Meningie road, and into 800 acres of the Prince's scrub. Luckily a fire break had been ploughed on the more open, southern side of the scrub, so the fire was stopped there, only burning about 25 acres of scrub.

However, it continued burning east and south of the road, and burnt about 25,000 acres in that direction. The average size house block then being about half an acre.

Thankfully no livestock were lost with the only casualty being me; however, lots of fencing and grass were burnt. The neighbours, who suffered about two-thirds of the total damage, were very good about not asking for reparation, and we had lots of help to repair the fencing.

My two brothers in law, Chris and Patrick Hill, came down from Adelaide and helped put out spot fires and did other odd jobs.

James recalls that soon after this they all had lunch at the Naval and Military Club in Adelaide. During the meal they discussed what happened, particularly to me, and they all started to cry, with tears pouring down their cheeks. The rest of the dining room was amazed that a table of grown men were brought to tears.

It is recorded by the hospital staff that I walked into the hospital and was able to talk. James lifted me onto the barouche. Brian Symon and his staff immediately decided that the first thing to do was to hydrate me. They inserted needles and tubes into my feet so that fluid could be pumped into my body.

As I was by this time in a lot of pain, they also gave me an appropriate dose of morphine. In fact, I believe I was under the impression until recently that Brian saved my life by only giving me lots and lots of morphine!

Some other measures were performed to stabilise me, and they then ordered a helicopter to take me to the Royal Adelaide Hospital, which came complete with its own retrieval Doctor and Registered Nurse.

At that time there was no facility for landing on the hospital roof, so I was unloaded from the helicopter and transferred into an ambulance at a nearby parkland and transported to the hospital. When I arrived at the Royal Adelaide Hospital at 7 pm I was assessed as having 3rd degree burns to 55-65% of my body, in the upper region. They also found that my airways were swollen and partially blocked. Because of this I was sent to the intensive care unit.

The size of a burn is measured as a percentage of total body surface area (TBSA) affected by partial thickness or full thickness burns.

All new burns patients are assessed for the following risk factors for chances of survival. The factors are:

1. Degree of burns – in my case 55-65% of 3rd degree burns
2. Age – in my case 64 years
3. Requiring a ventilator – 40%

So that left me with a total of 169% risk.

No doctor can remember a patient that has survived with this level of risk. There have been some with more burns, but because they were younger they had better survival rates.

So, it seemed very unlikely that I should survive. But I did. So maybe a look at my previous life might help suggest why.

Chapter 2
Family background

I was born in 1926, the youngest of four children, and we lived in a lovely old single storey house, number 30 Dequetteville Terrace, Kent Town.

By 1932, we each had a bedroom of our own, a big garden to play in, and a tennis court. When I was very young, we had a cook, house maid and a parlour maid. In those days my Dad was called Father by his children and my Mum called Mother. It seems quaint now, does it not?

My father, Leslie Harvey, was of Scottish descent. His grandparents lived on a farm near Aberdeen in Scotland and his father immigrated to Australia as a young man.

My grandfather, James Harvey, did well in the business world, looking after the business affairs of the Barr-Smith family. My father fought in World War 1 in the British Army Royal Artillery, thankfully ending up still alive and with the rank of Major.

After the war he became a partner in M. G. Anderson and Co., who were agents for the Orient Line of passenger ships that ran between England and Australia.

They were large passenger ships of 20,000 tons, and together with the P & O Line were the major means of travel between the two continents.

He had other business interests, such as starting the first tuna fishing factory in the Eyre Peninsula, and was a Director and then Chairman of the Portland Cement Company.

Although he had wide interests, he was shy and retiring, never seeking the lime light, reserved, and quiet, but a great father to me, especially in later life.

My mother Llevelys, was of Welsh descent and her grandfather, Edwin Thomas, had a newspaper business in London. He came to Australia with his family, one of the first to arrive on the ship named the "Aquitaine". He brought with him printing presses and started the first Adelaide newspaper, "The Register".

His son, Jabez Thomas, who I think worked at "The Register", bought number 30 Dequetteville Terrace, and later sold it to my father.

So, my mother would have spent most of her life in that house. As I have said, it was a lovely old house and the four Harvey children, Alison, Alain, Herries, and I all grew up there in a caring and quiet environment. I was the youngest, and never bullied by the others and I was allowed to join in with my sibling's pursuits.

At the age of nine I was sent as a monthly boarder to Wykeham Preparatory School, for boys only, at Belair. An unusual boarding school, run by Mr & Mrs Hutchison who did all the teaching. It had extensive grounds, an oval and a swimming pool, and several acres of scrub.

I think I spent my first day crying, but eventually settled into the school routine. There were only about 25 boys in 1935 but the standard of learning was not high. We were not made to remember what we were taught, so nearly everybody did very badly at the end of term exams.

School numbers were too small to compete with other schools, but we learnt about football and cricket and how to swim. Boxing was also part of school life, and we had boxing tournaments to which parents were invited. I remember seriously embarrassing my father when I was badly beaten by Tom Legoe in the final, and burst into floods of tears. Tom later went on to be the middleweight champion in the Australian Navy.

At the end of 1937, school numbers were down to eight students, so the school closed.

I then went on to the junior school of Geelong Grammar School in Victoria, partly I think because some of my best friends were going there. I spent two enjoyable years there – 1938 and 1939 – learning a lot more and retaining it, and enjoying playing football and athletics. This came to an abrupt end in 1939 when World War II started.

Petrol rationing was introduced, so Geelong Grammar became more distant and remote from Adelaide. My parents thought I would be better off closer to home, so in 1940 I went to St Peter's College in Adelaide SA.

I had a happy time there for four years, doing reasonably well at school work, and matriculating in 1943. Because I was not naturally a naughty boy, I avoided any punishments by the masters.

In my last year – 1943 – I was in the first tennis team, spent two years in the first football team, and came runner up in the College Cup for athletics. I was also made Vice Captain of the School.

Disaster struck in the middle of 1943, when my elder brother Alain, a bomber and Pathfinder Pilot in the Royal Airforce, was shot down and killed over Germany. For many months I was silent and reserved, determined to join the Airforce at the end of the year. But this was not to be. One of the requirements of the medical exam for the services was fitness to go to the tropics. I had a severe case of acne and was ruled out by a medical exam on those grounds.

Bitterly disappointed, I entered the University of Adelaide in Agricultural Science. This was because my father had become the owner of a large property of 16,000 acres, called Yalkuri, on the Narrung Peninsula.

Its southern boundary was the Coorong, its western boundary Lake Alexandrina.

The Harvey children used to spend most of their school holidays down there, sailing, riding, and shooting rabbits. I thought it was paradise.

My father thought it would be a good idea if I had some knowledge of agriculture, hence this course at the University.

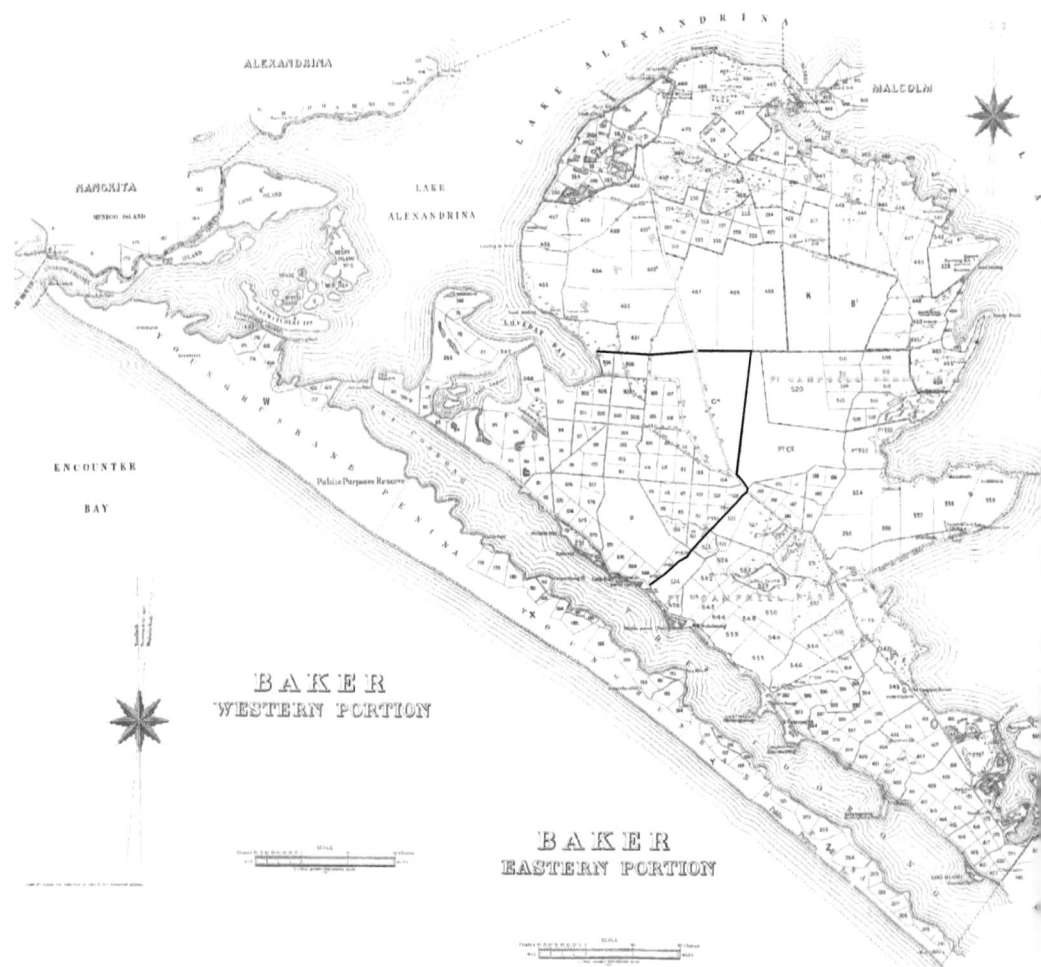

Map of Lake Alexandrina and the Coorong, showing Yalkuri in the South-West corner of the Narrung Peninsula.

Chapter 3

Life after university

The next four years I try not to remember. First, I went from being a fairly important person at school, to a non-entity. Second, I could not get over the fact that I could not join the services and go to the war. Most of my friends were doing this and I was not. I felt like a third-rate citizen, and so became even more introverted and reserved. This was not helped by the fact that one of the first-year subjects was Botany 1. This involved the fundamentals of plants, which I found extremely dull.

Time went on, I got to know the fellow students in my year and managed to pass the final fourth year with a credit grade.

CSIRO at this time – 1947 – were funding a lot of work in wool research. I applied for a job called "Supervisor of Fleece Testing". This involved going to selected South Australian Merino studs and taking wool samples of their top sheep. These were then taken back to the Research Centre at Roseworthy College where I was based. I carried out various measurements on these samples, such as staple length and strength, to determine their merit. Though it was important, I found it very repetitive and boring. I was living in a small house at Roseworthy with three other graduates who were also working at the College. The home was infested with possums, which lived in the ceiling and ran across it all night.

Meanwhile my father had purchased 8,000 acres of scrub North of Bordertown in the upper South East for seven shillings and six pence per acre. There was a little cleared land, about 200 acres.

He suggested to me in 1948 to go there and manage the clearing of the property, called Berangwee. I accepted gladly, and then began a very different life.

Berangwee then had 200 acres of sown pasture, and a house in which Laurie Brine and his family lived. His job at the time was picking up burnt logs and sticks after the burning of the logged scrub. This was a monotonous job, at which he was very good, using a horse and chain to drag them into heaps for further burning.

The house was on the Pinnaroo-Bordertown Road, which at that time for the first ten miles south from the house, was atrocious. Sandy in parts in the summer and waterlogged in clay patches in the winter, it was a nightmare for any conventional car. I do not know how Laurie survived there for so long.

As there was no other house for me, the old Yalkuri church (made of weatherboard) was dismantled and half of it brought down to Berangwee. It was rebuilt near the northern side of the cleared land.

It was one room, with a bed and a "Metters No. 2" wood stove. There was a windmill, dam, and trough nearby. I washed in the trough (not very often, because it was so cold in the mornings). I learnt to cook on the wood stove, having not cooked for myself before, but there were plenty of Mallee roots for the stove which kept it hot.

I had one of the earliest Land Rovers, so I would go into Bordertown once a week to purchase stores, not more often because petrol rationing was still happening. When I first arrived, I knew nobody in the district, not a soul. It was quite a daunting time in my life.

1948 was very much a different life, because I had no practical experience of farming. Basically, I could ride a horse, drive a car, and was physically fit at the age of 22, but that was all I had.

To achieve the land clearing program, my father and I formed a partnership, L. M. Harvey and Son. This company owned a D4 Caterpillar tractor, with a huge log to knock down the scrub, a Majestic disc plough, harrows, and a disc seeder.

The drivers of the machinery, were initially living at Laurie Brine's house, and the program was for 500 acres per year to be cleared, ploughed and then seeded with pasture.

CSIRO had been testing these soils for deficiency, and had found they were very low in the elements copper and zinc. With these elements added to superphosphate, it made the soil very productive, and with good rainfall, transformed this desert country into good productive grazing land.

We needed sheep to graze these pastures, so first I erected a set of primitive sheep yards, made out of Mallee, as steel products were not available at this time. Next, I bought a line of five year old ewes from Baldina Station at Burra, which were based on Collinsville blood.

I needed rams for these ewes so Alan Johnson, Head of Stud Stock at Dalgetys, suggested I buy rams from Collinsville, perhaps the foremost South Australian stud at that time, owned and managed by Art Collins.

Alan took me to Collinsville, Mount Bryan, where we had lunch with Mr & Mrs Collins. Afterwards we were taken to the sheep yards to see a pen of twelve rams. They were some of the worst rams I have ever seen. I think Art thought, "here's a new breeder, who won't know anything about rams".

I had some experience looking at good rams during my time at Roseworthy as Supervisor of Fleece Testing. I suggested to Mr Collins, "these were a terrible lot of rams, and were insulting a potential buyer, I may have to go elsewhere".

"Oh", said Art, "I'll see if we can do better." We went around to another corner of the yard, where there was a pen of very good rams, with careful selection, I had just what I wanted. So, I swallowed my pride, and thus began many years of purchasing Collinsville rams. This was much to the relief of Alan Johnson.

Meanwhile, in 1950, I married Jenny Hill, the daughter of the then Saints Headmaster, John Hill. An Army Colonel and strict disciplinarian, I liked him very much.

I had built a small house north of my hut, into which Jenny and I moved in late 1950. Jenny, aged 18, was very much a city girl, so it must have been a huge shock to have to cook on a wood stove, have a kerosene refrigerator and a petrol-driven washing machine, which was very temperamental. I always had to be near the house on Monday mornings in case it broke down.

We started off with no electric power, using Tilley kerosene lamps. A few years later I bought a diesel power plant, which gave us light but no power for irons or a washing machine. We still had petrol rationing, so there was still only once a week trips to Bordertown to shop for food. If you forgot the bread, too bad – for a week.

But Jenny coped with this very well, and we gradually made some friends in the district. We played tennis with the Lowan Vale team on Saturdays, and Jenny became a leading actress in the Bordertown Dramatic Society.

We had four children, two girls and two boys, and they all went to the Bordertown Primary School, except David, who was too young. They were very hardworking and happy times. The Pinnaroo Road that we were on, as I have said previously, was terrible and not useable by 2-wheel-drive vehicles.

Myself and other landholders began agitating for improvement, until finally it became a graded dirt road to our gate, and then many years later became bitumen.

The result was the Lowan Vale area became known to the rest of the Tatiara District, and were granted a seat on the Tatiara District Council. I was the first Councillor.

After some years, I became Chairman of the Finance Committee and then Chairman of the Council at the young age of 36. I enjoyed it all very much, and created a friendly link between two major factions in the Council, Bordertown and Keith.

I introduced a firm called "Personnel Administration" to the Council, to try to update procedures. This was a great success, making the Council very much more efficient, without huge disruption.

Berangwee Homestead, 1950

Chapter 4

Onto Yalkuri

In 1961, Keith Bakewell, the Manager of Yalkuri, announced he wanted to retire at the end of 1962. The Bakewell family had bought Yalkuri from the Bowmans in 1918 which was a part of "Campbell Park". Keith and his brother Don became the joint managers. They developed the property, built houses, woolsheds and yards, and spent and borrowed a lot of money. They became unstuck in the depression, so other shareholders were brought in, including my father, in 1929.

By 1932 L. M. Harvey owned Yalkuri, except for a small share held by Keith and Don Bakewell. Soon after this, my father decided one manager was enough, and Don Bakewell left.

Keith became the manager for nearly 30 years, and a very good one. Even-tempered and thoughtful, he kept up with the times and was one of nature's gentlemen. He taught me a lot.

I had been a Director of Yalkuri for some years, so it seemed that now was the time for me to take over the management. It was decided that we would sell Berangwee, so our family could move to Yalkuri at the beginning of 1963.

I resigned from the Council during the middle of 1962, and started organising our departure. I decided to take our Merino flock to Yalkuri, selling the Corriedale flock, in the hope that the Merinos would make more money.

I sold our small Hereford breeding herd, and put Berangwee on the market. It was very slow, but we finally sold the cleared half to Bruce Sinclair. The northern scrub end was sold some years later.

In January 1963 we moved to Yalkuri, taking with us Bruce Hayes and his family, who went to the Lake House on Loveday Bay. So, ended a happy period of my life. I liked the Tatiara, its people, and the way of life that we had led. It was now about to change.

Yalkuri was very different. The staff composed a manager, an overseer, and about 5 or 6 station hands. Berangwee had a manager and one station hand. Berangwee was making a small profit. Yalkuri was making a loss, but why? The answer was rabbits.

During my last year on the Tatiara Council, the Department of Lands had appointed a new Chief Vermin Officer, from CSIRO Wildlife Division, called John Bromell. He was an expert on rabbit control. As soon as he arrived, he toured the state looking for suitable members of a proposed Vermin Advisory Committee. They would look at ways of controlling vermin, principally rabbits and dingoes, with the priority on rabbits. He asked me to join this Committee.

Now we had some rabbits, but not many, on Berangwee, and I had been able to almost eradicate them by ripping the burrows and fumigating the ones that reopened. They were not a serious threat.

John Bromell wanted a property to conduct trials on bait material for the poison *1080*, so I suggested that when I went to Yalkuri he could have an area to do this, if he would plan a poisoning program for the property.

Let me explain the problem on Yalkuri. It was 16,000 acres in area, 10,000 of which were arable open grassland, 6,000 acres being swamp or scrub. On the 10,000 acres of open land, rabbit counts showed there were about 500,000 rabbits. That is a huge number of rabbits. Warrens were being regularly ripped, and at least four station hands were trapping rabbits at night and selling them (their day work suffered as they were up half the night). There were also four full time professional rabbit trappers, each allocated their own area. But all this time and effort hardly made a dent in the rabbit population, so the rabbits were munching away at the grass, hardly leaving enough feed to carry the same amount of livestock as at the beginning, in spite of large improvements made in the pastures.

Yalkuri could not carry on making a loss. Bromell proposed that we poison the whole cleared area with this new poison called *1080*. It had been used very effectively in NSW and Victoria. If this proved successful on such a large farm, run commercially, then the whole of South Australia could adopt it. It was by-far the biggest challenge I had faced to date.

The details of this program are described in the book "Yalkuri", but I might highlight what happened. We needed two men, each driving a tractor with a baitlayer. They started on the Eastern side of the property and worked towards the West. They put out three "free feeds" of oats every four days. Then a fourth feed of oats mixed with *1080* was done and covered a week later. This was followed up by a third man with a tractor and disc harrows ploughing in the burrows. Any holes that opened up were fumigated with carbon monoxide until no more holes were opened.

Spotlight counts before and after the poisoning on the first area done showed a rabbit kill of 90%, a very good result. On May 14th, 1963, 10,000 acres had been poisoned, all the cleared land. We had laid 2,000 miles of trail, and used more *1080* than the state of Victoria in this year. It was certainly the largest *1080* work undertaken on one property in this state, and probably in Australia.

It was an outstanding success. After the opening rains (which luckily occurred soon after we had finished), the feed grew without interruption and we wanted more stock.

As development and improvements went on, Yalkuri became a very profitable enterprise.

R. G. M. Harvey 1966.
Before going to the UK on a Nuffield Scholarship.

In 1966 I was granted a Nuffield Scholarship for 6 months in the UK studying farm management procedures. I learnt a lot, made many friends and contacts, and then came home.

By the year 1990, Yalkuri had 1,100 Aberdeen Angus breeding cows, and a share dairy with 300 cows. We were selling irrigated lucerne hay, and doing some cropping.

Besides all this, I was on the State Committee of CSIRO, and still on the Vermin Committee which became the Animal and Pest Plant Commission. I was Vice President of the Stock Owners Association. I was asked if I would be the Pastoral Consultant for four large properties in the New England area of NSW, owned by the Finance Corporation of Australia.

I was on the board of Koonoona Proprietors, a large Merino stud at Burra, and Pastoral Advisor to some properties in the Meningie area, South Australia. In the early 1970s I became a member of the St Peters College Council, and later the Chairman of its Finance and Executive Committee. But my main interest was still Yalkuri.

The Yalkuri Homestead, 1989.

R.G.M.H. at the new cattle yard, Yalkuri 1988.

R.H.M.H. feeding an Angus bull, Yalkuri 1988

R.G.M.H. Morning tea, burning fire breaks 1988.

The Harvey family:
Back row: James Harvey, Richard Harvey, Sue Harvey, Christina Gillingham, Russell Gillingham.
Front row: David Harvey, Jenny Harvey, Shylie MacIntosh, Cathie Harvey

Burning fire breaks in Kartoo scrub, 1988, Brendan Savage and R.G.M.H.

Burning fire breaks in Kartoo scrub, 1988

Chapter 5

Daughter-in-law recount

My daughter-in-law Sue Harvey (a registered nurse), told me the following story. She arrived at the Royal Adelaide Hospital with my accountant and friend Colin Ferguson. When I was offloaded to the burns unit, they were told to wait in an adjoining room where they could hear me talking. They asked the burns unit nurse who had brought them in if they could see me. "Oh no", said the nurse, "we are doing procedures with him at present, and putting him on a ventilator, so maybe see him later". Sue and Colin were still there at 1 am in the morning and finally the nurse suggested they go home and come back later the next morning.

Sue arrived the next morning and the same nurse (very reluctantly) agreed that she could see me. Sue responded, "I know why I was not allowed to see Richard last night, because you all thought he would die." "You were quite right, but miraculously he is still alive and talking, so you'd better come and see him," the nurse replied.

I was taken that morning to the intensive care unit where I remained for three weeks, nearly all the time unconscious.

Sue (bless her heart) came in to see me every morning. On one morning she noticed that my face had turned blue. She reported this to the duty sister who said, "Oh no, he is perfectly alright." "No, he's not", said Sue, "I've just lifted his head up – you'd better come look at him." "You are right, he is blue." Sue probably saved my life!

Because my airways were partially blocked, I was placed on a ventilator to breathe for me, and remained on this for about a week. Then the plastic surgeons Ian Leitch, Jim Katsaros, and Phillip Griffin, commenced debriding me – which I gather means removing burnt skin and putting back new skin taken from my legs.

In all, I had eleven trips to the operating theatre. The theatre sister in charge then was Sheila Kavanagh, who has risen to the head of the burns unit. She has been a great help to me in writing this story and is a wonderful person.

I first remember becoming conscious in the hospital, with the plastic surgeon in charge of the burns unit, Ian Leitch, standing over me and saying that he had heard from Graham Wilson, another surgeon, that I had been a prominent athlete at school.

That was probably meant to make me feel at ease, but I thought it was a bit academic at the time and drifted into unconsciousness. There was some concern about my mental state, but thankfully that did improve. I had a feeding tube for a period while I was on the ventilator, until I could swallow again when the ventilator was removed.

All this time when I was unconscious, I was having a series of extraordinary dreams. The one I remember best was being in a small aeroplane flying to New Guinea, with a beautiful girl sitting on my lap. The skies were a perfect blue and the rest I will leave to your imagination. Many years later I met Georgia Conte who looked exactly like the girl in the dream.

Chapter 6

The RAH

After three weeks in ICU, I was brought into the burns unit. This was an eight-bed unit with only one bathroom and one lavatory, which created a bit of a bottleneck.

I occupied the bed nearest to the nurse's station, because I was the most severely damaged patient and they could keep an eye on me.

Soon after my arrival there, my first conscious memory was of Ian Leitch standing over me and saying, "We took a lot of trouble over you, because you absolutely refused to die. Make sure you keep on trying."

Now I suspect that I was helped in this by having a fairly high tolerance to pain, and therefore the general agony was not so great. The unit had one special mattress which was soft and spongy with a lot of air holes that made lying on it with very raw skin much more bearable and promoted healing. After being given this mattress my life was infinitely more comfortable.

When I left the Royal Adelaide, I wondered if I could give the burns unit something for all the help they had given me. I decided on one of these mattresses, very expensive, but I'm sure a great help to future burns patients.

The next few weeks were devoted to the surgeons putting more skin on my burnt areas. This was before the days of artificial skin, so the new skin had to be taken from the parts of me that were not burnt. This was the legs and buttocks, and it was a slow process, because you have to let new skin regrow on this area for two weeks before you can take any more. I was not allowed a pillow, because that somehow did bad things, and if you have never slept without a pillow I can tell you it's difficult.

While my back was being done, I had to lie on my stomach for several weeks, which was also quite a test and very uncomfortable.

Apparently, you can only blush above the neck – so the composition of the skin above the neck is different to the rest of the body.

Because my face was badly burnt, the surgeons took skin from my scalp. In fact, I was scalped. This was a painful operation but very successful, because only my nose and lips still show evidence of the burns.

Generally, the hair follicles are below the outer skin line, so all my hair came back on my head (much to my relief) but some hairs started to grow in odd places such as cheeks and forehead. The nurses, and Jenny, really enjoyed plucking them out.

Other aspects of the burns unit: There were up to seven other patients in the burns unit, but we had very little contact with each other. Being in separate rooms, we were mostly kept, by circumstances of treatment and infection control, to our own room.

I cannot remember, in any way, the other patients during my stay there. Just before I left, I do remember an Abyssinian woman who was brought in, with horrific burns that were self-inflicted. Her husband was a doctor, they had come to Australia to make a new life, but she hated it. She had set herself alight as she did not wish to go on living. She died after a few days, and that really affected me. It was terrible, and I felt for her whole family.

Many of the burns patients were affected, not only physically but also mentally. It does create in some people a great mental strain, with anxiety and stress being a huge problem.

I was told of one man so affected that he reverted to childhood for his escape and now plays with his Hornby trains.

The hospital employed a psychiatrist while I was there, called Edith Miller. She came in to see me after a short time and asked what was troubling me mentally. My reply was the only trouble I had was to get better quickly, and she didn't believe me. She came back a week later, and asked me the same question. She got the same reply, so I had no need to see her again. Because I had no mental health problems I must have been a rare case.

The hospital staff asked me if I would be happy to speak to two other young male patients with burns. I agreed to do this, and they were brought in to see me as I was a good example of how to cope with stress. They seemed to benefit from this.

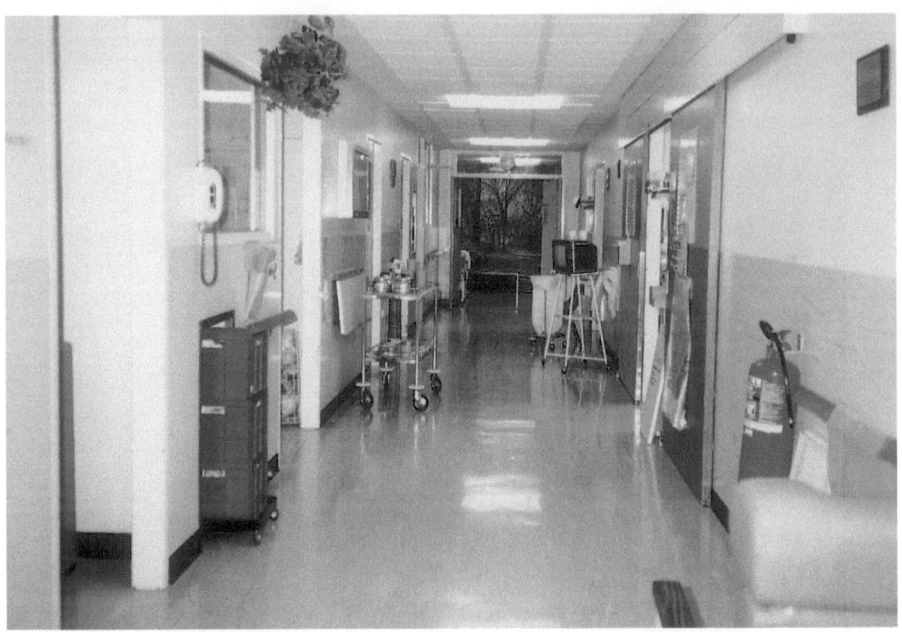

The Burns Unit, Royal Adelaide Hospital, 1990.

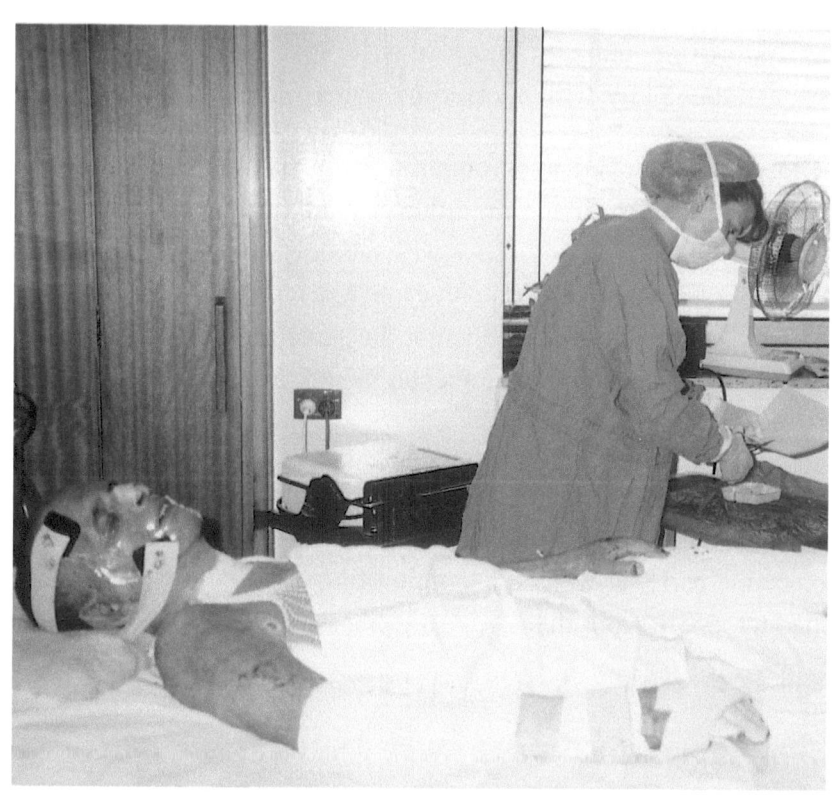

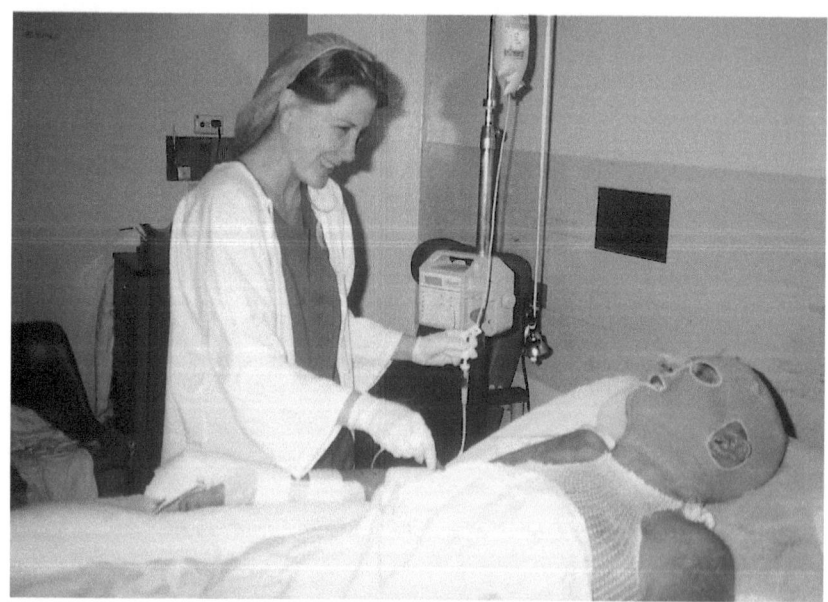

R.G.M.H. Burns Unit, Royal Adelaide Hospital, 1990.

The staff

The burns unit staff were quite outstanding, in their quality of nursing, care and attention to their patients.

When I arrived, Pam Stewart was in charge. Very able and efficient, by coincidence she was engaged to a neighbour of ours at Yalkuri. She married soon afterwards and left.

The next one was Anne Hill, again very good, and if things went wrong with a patient, she very quickly fixed it personally. She transferred to run another unit and Sheila Kavanagh took over to run the unit to the present day.

The nurses were all good, but of the ones I remember, Amanda comes to mind. She was very caring and great company, I have met her since. The first time on a bench in Melbourne Street, and then more recently in her and her husband's business next door to the Prospect Council Chambers.

I have been a Justice of the Peace since I was made one when I was Chairman of the Tatiara Council in 1962. I was asked if I would undertake Justice of the Peace duties at the Prospect Council.

A year or two later, we were invited by the Mayor to a dinner. Lo and behold, there was Amanda with her husband Tim, and we had a great reunion.

Then there was Rosie, very caring and down to earth, and David, who later obtained a degree in psychology.

One morning in a waking dream I said to David, "We must get down to the cattle yards straight away!" He kept his composure and agreed that it was very necessary. Needless to say, we did not leave the ward and go the cattle yards.

Then there was Moira, an attractive nurse who did parachute jumping.

Whilst in hospital, I was on a continuous morphine drip, inserted in my toe, which I needed for pain relief. One night, about 1 am, when Moira was looking after me, I asked her to hop into bed with me. That was the end of the morphine.

In the occupational therapy division, Margot Masters was in charge, but mostly I was treated by a Swede called Birgit Svens, tall and strong with very good skin. She helped me to get some movement back into my hands.

The head of the physiotherapy department was Margaret McMahon. She put me through many exercises to help me regain strength, particularly in my hands and arms which were very weak after no activity. One of the worst features of a long hospital stay is that you never know how well, or badly, you are progressing, because you get told nothing (or very little).

Margaret was a great help in giving me some idea of my future, in her quiet Irish way, and there were many other kind nurses who helped to make my stay more bearable.

Chapter 7

First stages of recovery

After the numerous skin graft operations (I think there were 17), all with full anaesthetics, I began the first tentative steps to getting better. It became apparent that one of the major problems was that my arms would not bend. With straight arms you cannot feed yourself, you cannot clean your teeth, or do many of the normal things that you take for granted.

The physiotherapist Michelle, assigned to rectify this, did her best to try and make them bend, but it always ended with me screaming in agony. In fact, every time I saw her come into the room, I said, "No please, not again".

This must have been quite distressing for her as well as me, so it was suggested that a psychologist called Kent, work on me with hypnosis and then the physio tries again when I am under hypnosis. Kent and I chatted about a lot of things, before he put me under, he was a pleasure to be with but alas, the result was the same – I woke up after a bit, feeling severe pain, with no result.

All this was happening while I was still bed-bound, not yet ready to get out, and still very weak. Somebody decided it would be a good idea to have an x-ray of my elbows to see if there was a bone problem. I was wheeled into an x-ray ward where I stayed for several hours, with nobody taking any notice of me. Finally, I attracted a nurse's attention to find out that I had been forgotten, went to the end of the queue and finally late in the afternoon had the x-ray taken. The results showed that both my upper and lower arm bones were fused together at the elbow, no doubt due to the intense heat at the time of the fire. No wonder my arms did not bend.

Just after this, an American plastic surgeon specialising in burns arrived from California. All unusual burns cases were wheeled into an inspection room and I was one of them.

Nurse David took me there and wished me luck. When the American came around to me, he looked at the x-rays and said I should have both elbows operated on at the same time (to save expense), and the bone cut away to free them. Ian Leitch had suggested I be referred to Michael Hayes, an orthopaedic surgeon. Michael had not done this operation before, in fact I was the first burns patient in Adelaide (if not in Australia) to have this problem.

Thank God, he sensibly refused to do both operations together, and suggested I should get some general strength back before he did the first one.

Because I had difficulty using cutlery for meals, a long spoon and fork was made for me, with which I could (with some difficulty), feed myself. They were about one and a half feet long, and took quite some getting used to. But at least I could feed myself – although not clean my teeth.

I had been complaining about teeth cleaning, fearing decay might set in, so Jenny arranged for my dentist Graham Mount to come and see me. There was a room in the hospital with an ancient dentist's chair in it. I was taken to it with Graham Mount in attendance. The chair was operated by pedal-power, so Graham lifted me up but found he had gone too far, so he pushed the down pedal and I crashed with a jolt toward the floor. Finally, he got it right and inspected and cleaned my teeth, and fortunately found no problems after six weeks of neglect. He then told the person in charge that somebody must clean my teeth every day, and do the same with other patients if they themselves could not do it. And it happened, which was a very good result and a credit to Graham Mount, and Jenny for getting him. She had done a wonderful job in this, and many ways, visiting me every day, which was not easy.

Second stage of recovery

After many weeks, it was now time to get out of bed. After so many weeks lying mostly on my back, it was a major effort. At first, standing up I felt dizzy and nearly fell over, but the nurse saved me. I walked three steps to a chair into which I collapsed. But even sitting down was an endurance, so after a while I rang the bell, and when the nurse came I asked if I could get back to bed. Well, she gave me the rounds of the kitchen, told me I was lucky to be able to get up, and to stop whingeing and complaining. You can imagine how I felt by this tirade, but it taught me a lesson. Never complain! So, after that I never did, which was a good thing, because I was looked on as a sort of freak. And she did put me back to bed.

I slowly became more mobile, even walking up and down the passage a number of times a day. When Ian Leitch passed me, he would say, "Keep it up, and keep doing more each day, even if it hurts".

I was getting better, but there was a short period in the middle of my stay when things were bad. I had picked up a staphylococcal infection, which made me feel so sick and terrible that it was the only time that I really wanted to die.

Fortunately, Anne Hill, who was in charge at the time, was alerted, and spent a lot of time with me, giving me antibiotics and trying to cheer me up. After several days, her care worked, and I slowly felt better, but I think I was closer to death than at any other time.

I was taken up to the OT department, where Birgit gave me hand massages and other exercises, regaling me with the virtues of the ski slopes of Sweden.

I also went to the Physiotherapy department where Margaret McMahon worked on me, and tried to strengthen my pathetically weak arms and legs, both of which looked like matchsticks.

She also looked after my mental wellbeing. I had found a book by Joan Collins, which I was reading with glee while waiting for her one day. She came by, saw me reading this, and said, "Richard, stop reading that trash immediately!", so I did. She was a great woman.

Soon after my leaving the Royal Adelaide Hospital, Margaret suggested that I might give a number of lectures to final year Physiotherapy students at the University.

I agreed to do this and fronted up to 30 or 40 fourth-year students. They looked at me rather as a museum piece, but I started up and you could have heard a pin drop while I was talking. I think they had never experienced such a dramatic lecture in their lives. Anyway, it was a great success and I continued doing this for the next 2 years until Margaret left her position, and I really quite enjoyed myself.

Meanwhile, because I was getting better, I was moved to a room further away from the nurse's station, until I came to be in the bed furthest away from the nurse station. It is quite amazing now, but I felt lonely and a bit rejected, feeling that they all did not care anymore! Of course, I was wrong.

Chapter 8

Visitors

The Royal Adelaide Hospital must be one of the most difficult places to see a patient. Parking is (or was) a nightmare. There was an open car park where it was often difficult during the day to find a park, and it was some distance from the burns unit, not good if it was raining. There were no other parking areas within reasonable distance. There is now a car park building, but it seems to be mostly full during the day.

Jenny came in to see me most days and nights, and provided great comfort and support. My needs were few, but visitors were a big lift to my mental attitude. I think Jenny thought I should not have too many, but I enjoyed having them, and none outstayed their welcome.

My son James and his wife Sue also came to visit nearly every day. My daughter Shylie and her husband Mark Mackintosh were living in London at the time, but as soon as they heard about my being burnt they came to Adelaide. When they arrived, I was still in intensive care on a ventilator and there was doubt about my survival. They stayed for four days by which time I was pronounced out of immediate danger. They went back to London where they were both working, but Shylie decided to come back just after Christmas for a further visit.

My son David came to see me as often as he could, but living in the country 100 miles away, meant that this did not occur often. I was always very glad to see him and hear how the dairy was going.

My sister Alison, who I had not seen a lot of during the preceding years, realised that her only surviving family member may be on the brink. She used to make a number of visits during the week, mostly on her way to the University, where she was doing first year Greek, just for interest!

I might add that at the end of second year she had to give up the idea of a further degree because she ran out of lecturers. She was 72 at the time, a truly remarkable person. Her intellect was way above mine, but I really enjoyed her visits.

In 1990, I had for some years been Chairman of the Finance and Executive Committee, of the Council of Governors of St Peter's College. As the President role was not executive, many decisions fell to me.

Consequently, my sudden absence caused a little dismay, and some of my first visitors were Tony Schinkfield, and Ray Stanley, the Headmaster and his Deputy. I gather after their visit they told somebody I was very ill but my voice was the same.

The President of the Council, Keith Rayner, had just become the Primate of the Anglican Church of Australia, and had moved to Melbourne. His place was temporarily taken at the school by Bruce Rosier, the Bishop of Willochra. I was very touched that Bruce came to see me several times when he must have been frantically busy, coping with his new responsibilities. He is a very able and humble man, now a Parish Priest in Adelaide.

There were others. John Bromell, Richard Downward, Kevin Gogler, from the Animal and Pest Plants Commission. My godson Bob Legoe, Michael Cudmore, and even the man who started the fire Brendan Savage. The latter was very nervous, wondering how I would feel about him, but it was not his fault and I was very glad to see him. There were others that I have not mentioned, but I was glad to see them all.

Diet

When I arrived at the burns unit from intensive care, my throat was still very swollen and restricted. The only nourishment I could take, apart from the drips I had been having, was ice-cream.

Now ice-cream had always been a favourite of mine, but imagine several weeks of only ice-cream for breakfast, lunch and dinner. By the end of it, I could hardly look ice-cream in the face.

Gradually my throat returned to normal, and so other soft foods could be eaten, and I thought the hospital (considering its size) provided good food.

R.G.M.H. taking in the air, Royal Adelaide Hospital, January 1991.

Clothing

While the skin graft operations were taking place, and for a healing period afterwards, my only clothing was my standard white hospital cotton gown, with tabs at the back.

But from then on, it was necessary to compress the burnt areas, to stop the skin expanding into big red, permanent, scarred welts. Because I was burnt over most of my body, I was required to wear a tight cotton compression suit over all my body, which was zipped up at the front.

I was supplied two of these, as the suits were changed every day and washed. Vastly uncomfortable, they compressed the burnt areas and I wore mine for about 12 months. Then on my face I wore a face mask of the same material. These masks were all made in Ireland because I understand their origin goes back to the days of the Irish Republican Army (IRA) who wore them to hide their identity.

Plastic masks were just being tried as a better option, so my Occupational Therapist had one made for me. It was even more horrible to wear than the cotton ones, because in hot weather (which it was then) they did not breathe, so I sweated badly inside the mask. I only lasted two days with mine.

I was shown how necessary all this was, by a photograph of a young girl of 16 who refused to wear one, saying it spoiled her appearance. The photo showed a very bad red raised scar across one cheek, and I'm sure she regretted her decision for the rest of her life.

This convinced me that I must keep wearing these suits and masks for as long as necessary – which was about 12 months. I am glad now that I persevered, because I was left with scarred skin but no red welts.

Last days in the burns unit

By the beginning of March 1991, I was getting much better. I was able to go back to the flat at Walkerville with Jenny for a couple of weekends, which certainly was a welcome change of scene. Finally, it was decided by Ian Leitch that I could go to a rehabilitation hospital, Kiandra.

The Physiotherapist there, Tanya, was given instructions about exercises for me, and the head nurse Sue was also told how to handle my burns.

March the 15th was my last day at the Royal Adelaide, and the burns unit staff gave me a farewell party in the staffroom. Most of the senior nursing staff were present. Anne Hill, David, Newton, Amanda, Rosie, Moira, Sheila, and Kate. There was champagne, and lots of cakes – a truly wonderful send off.

Chapter 9

Kiandra Hospital

After a weekend at the flat in Walkerville, on Monday the 18th March we drove to Kiandra Hospital in Prospect. We were met by Jeremy Syme, the Director of nursing and CEO. By coincidence, I had known him at Meningie, where he was the CEO at the hospital there, and I was on the hospital board. It was good to see him again, a friendly, efficient operator.

Later in the day I had my first physiotherapy session with Tanya. She was very competent, and we became great friends. She certainly greatly helped to get my strength back, with two physiotherapy sessions a day, and later recommended me for a physiotherapy award for trying!

I also now had a new Occupational Therapist in Belinda from Focus. She worked on my fingers (which still had very little movement), twice a day, and did a great job with them.

I still needed to go the Royal Adelaide Hospital on a regular basis to see Margaret McMahon. I had been fitted with special compression gloves at the Royal Adelaide, and a second, better, compression suit was fitted as well.

On March 22nd I was back at the Royal Adelaide Hospital being fitted with two dynamic elbow splints. The idea was that I could get more movement in my elbows, but I do not think they were of much benefit because my elbows were still fused.

The general routine was Belinda giving me hand and finger exercises in the morning, in the afternoon Tanya giving me physiotherapy, then into the Kiandra hydrotherapy pool trying to swim as much as I could.

A regular weekly visitor was John Bromell, the CEO of the State Vermin Authority, of which I was a founding member. He was a great friend of mine and kept me up to date on recent happenings, assuming I would be back with them before long.

Other frequent visitors were Nan Warden, Doctor Graham Wilson, a surgeon at the Royal Adelaide, Tony Schinkfield, Headmaster of St Peter's College, and Ian Lloyd, who succeeded me as Chairman of the Executive Committee of the Council of Governors of St Peters, and later became Chairman of the Council. There were many other welcome visitors.

Kiandra was a more relaxed atmosphere than the Royal Adelaide. I had more freedom, going for walks (though short ones) and plenty of resting time. I do not remember mixing with other patients there, however all the nurses were friendly and helpful, and I got to know some of them quite well.

I am not sure how many operations I had at the Royal Adelaide, but I think it was 17. By now, both my eyelids were drooping and needed an operation to fix them.

Ian Leitch decided that early April 1991, while at Kiandra, would be a good time to do them. As you can imagine, the thought of another operation was pretty daunting. Finally, on April 29th I was taken to the Ashford Hospital and he operated on them there.

I was in hospital for three days to recover, my left eyelid was completely successful, the right one nearly so. Then I was taken back to Kiandra. I was still wearing my compression bodysuit and my facemask. They were not comfortable, but by this time I was used to them.

My fingers, under Belinda's treatment, had improved well in movement, though the middle finger of my right hand was still very stiff. Tanya's physiotherapy twice daily had improved my general body movement, particularly my shoulders, but the elbows were still fused, and so both arms were straight with no bend at the elbow. All this treatment was still supervised by Margaret McMahon and Brigit at the Royal Adelaide, to whom I paid weekly visits to check my progress.

Finally, at the end of April, Ian Leitch decided I could leave Kiandra and go home.

Chapter 10
Going home

Home was now a house in North Adelaide, built in the late 1800's. Jenny died of cancer in October 1992. I married Tess Cowan, from Poltalloch, a property not far from Yalkuri in 1993.

When I came out of Kiandra hospital, I was still wearing a compression suit, and I still couldn't bend my elbows. Dr Hayes also suggested that a nurse from an agency should be provided to help me, and to look after the compression suits and masks. Tess and I agreed that help was needed, so Kiandra called a Nursing Agency for potential help with day to day management. Alex Reynolds a Registered Nurse came to help.

She showered, dressed and fed me every day for nearly a year, including washing the compression suits and cleaning out my ears. In fact, because my ears had been burned, she only knew that the ear bud was in too deep when I started coughing as an automated bodily response, and said "Oy, that'll do", in response to which we both started laughing. We could not have had a better person. She did a great job and provided a new and vital life in my existence which physically and mentally stimulated me.

After she left we maintained intermittent contact, until we were asked to her wedding to Wally Conte, a detective in the police force. She had a baby Georgia, and nine years later she divorced. We ran in to her at a coffee shop in North Adelaide some years later and by that time she had divorced, and I was able to help her with some budgeting. We met monthly for several years after that.

When Tess became ill in 2015, I asked for her help, which she gladly gave looking after Tess, until Tess died several months later. The day after, she rang me and said, "Richard would you like me to cook breakfast for you". A truly wonderful offer, and she has been doing it ever since.

Just before Tess died, Tess heard about a small house that was for sale quite close to us. We looked at it with Tess, and Alex is now living there. My life has been truly blessed.

I had met Wally Conte once or twice before, but the next meeting was quite unique. My son David had asked me to lunch at the Club, and it was the first time I had been out in public all alone since hospital. I was naturally apprehensive about how people would feel about my facial disfigurement. My lips were large and swollen, and my nose had gaps in the nostrils. Any other burns effects on my body were covered up by the uncomfortable suits.

I went into the city and was walking down Grenfell St. when a car veered into the curb near me, and out jumped Wally Conte. He said, "How nice to see you again Richard. You are looking so well, and walking strongly." Well that gave me a big lift.

David and I had lunch at the club, and on our way into another room for coffee, we passed a table of six senior club members that I knew. They all stood up and said, "Glad to see you back Richard". Now that really was a wonderful thing for me, and from then on, I was quite comfortable with meeting people. The only group that used to stop and stare, were very young children, but why shouldn't they. To them I looked "different" and I understood.

I had ongoing issues with my elbows. In 1991 Michael Hayes had to operate on both elbows and physiotherapy and hand exercises would still go on under Tanya and Belinda. In August, Michael Hayes decided I was fit enough to have my right elbow operated on. He had not done this operation before, but I went to Ashford Hospital where he successfully cut away bone to allow the elbow joint to move.

The operation was a success, I could bend my right arm fully, but I could not fully straighten it. This however did not matter at all, because the bending fully gave me the ability to operate normally for the first time for nearly a year. It was essential that the elbow get immediate and regular physiotherapy. Michael called on Shylie Davidson, a senior physiotherapist at Sports Med, to do this. I was glad to see her because she was a close friend of my daughter Shylie Mackintosh, who had trained with her at the University.

Shylie Davidson started immediately to exercise my arm but unfortunately this caused some of the stitches to snap, causing a bloody mess underneath. Michael was summoned, stitched it up again, and luckily all was well. In a month the wound had healed but the exercises went on for a period.

Michael operated on my left elbow in September 1991, which was also a success, with no problems afterwards. Shylie continued with physiotherapy for another month until both my arms were operating freely. I was now feeling much better physically, walking a lot, and life seemed to return to near normality.

One final operation was needed on my right hand. I could use my thumb and forefinger well, was able to write, but the other three fingers were nearly useless, particularly my middle finger.

So, one more operation, the 22nd, happened at Sports Med, where a private hospital had just been built. Michael inserted an artificial joint in my middle finger and tried to help movement in the other two. I had a little more movement after this, but not much.

At the end of November, I saw Ian Leitch for the last time as his patient, and he said I would soon be able to discard wearing the compression suit and the mask, because my grafts had sufficiently healed. You cannot imagine my glee at this pronouncement, I felt like having a ceremonial bonfire of the offending garments which came off forever in early

December. Soon after this, Alex Reynolds left, as I was capable of doing everything for myself. I was sad when she went.

The only problem I still had was a drooping right eyelid, which the last eye operation had not cured. In the middle of 1992 I went to Dr Gary Davis, a very respected eye surgeon. He operated on the eyelid, my 23rd operation. It was completely successful.

I was now as physically fit after burns, as I was ever likely to be, and grateful I was finally over all the operations. I had to be careful not to expose my skin to the sun for more than short periods. I could not close the fingers of both hands enough to hold a golf club, so golf was out – although I did try once. My right shoulder was still limited in movement, only allowing me to serve at tennis with lollipops. I had returned to nearly normal health, with luckily no brain damage.

Chapter 11

Life after burns

I had already given up farming. I had given Yalkuri over to my two sons, James and David. James continued on with the same farming mix and had appointed his first manager Bruce Moulds, then Dennis Chandler, and finally his eldest son Henry.

David continued dairying, and became a very successful organic dairy farmer. He is now also the managing partner in Clifton Hills, a cattle station north of Maree, and I think the second largest in the world.

How should my life change after burns? There were clearly major changes needed.

First, my pastoral consulting work. Two of my largest outside commitments had ended in 1979-1980. The first was my membership of the research committee of the Australia wool board. Dr Bede Morris and I had been suggesting that not all funds go to CSIRO as previously but to other worthy organisations such as research into Calici Virus for rabbit control. This met the ire of CSIRO, so Sir Ewen Waterman asked me to resign from the committee which I did.

Secondly by this time the finance corporation of Australia (FCA) was in trouble and collapsed. The four pastoral properties owned by FCA in the New England area of NSW were beginning to show reasonable profits. I would like to think this was due to my help as pastoral advisor, particularly in the case of Paradise, one of the FCA properties of 12,000 acres which had a rich volcanic soil, and only required cheap dressings of sulphur rather than expensive superphosphate.

However, I was asked to sell the properties which I eventually did to a banker in Ohio USA.

Michael Elliott's large property, Naranga, which fronted the Coorong, had been purchased by a group led by Colin Ferguson's clients. I was retained as the pastoral consultant. This was again sold to a local farmer, Peter Saint, during my burns period, so my consultancy there finished.

Colin Ferguson also had a group of Doctors and Dentists who purchased Wanderaby near Meningie in the 1980's. I was their pastoral advisor and appointed Tim Lewis as Manager. This property we developed, but was sold in about 1991 to Perry Gunner when the previous group wanted retirement money. I did not continue with Gunner.

The Brookman property Rupari had been part of Yalkuri, but when I took over, my sister Alison was given Rupari, a much smaller farm. Her husband, David Brookman, the Agriculture Minister in the Playford Government, asked me to be their pastoral advisor. When he died in the late 1990s the property was sold, and I was no longer involved. So really after this time that part of my life was completed unrelated to me being burned.

Then there was St Peters College. By 1992, I had been on the school council for 17 years, the last few as chairman of the executive and finance committee.

This meant that I had responsibility for a lot of council decisions, as the chairman of the council was the Archbishop of Adelaide who was not really close to the running of the school. I decided it was time I resigned, so in July 1991 I went to my last council meeting dressed in my compression suit. This created a bit of a stir, but helped to make them agree to accept my resignation.

I remained for a short time as a member of the water resources tribunal, which decided the allocation and amount of water licences in South Australia.

Tess and I were spending part of our time at Poltalloch, managed by her son Chris Cowan. We had purchased a few blocks of Poltalloch land, so I decided to start a small Aberdeen Angus bull breeding herd of cattle.

This was a performance recorded herd, which is a herd that has a history of having good calving ability, and we provided bulls for Poltalloch and sold a few to outside buyers. This went on until I was 80 years old, when Tess said she thought I was too old to be with bulls in the cattle yard.

We sold the herd to Poltalloch and Tess was probably right. I had also been helping Chris with cattle work and advice for some years, but I thought it was a good time to quit.

This ended my days as a true farmer.

I remained on the Animal and Pest Plant Commission until I was 70, when I resigned.

Soon afterward I was awarded an AM as a member of the Order of Australia. This was for my work on rabbits, and as a pastoral consultant. I think the successful program of being the first large property to poison rabbits with *1080* in South Australia was my greatest achievement. From approximately 500,000 rabbits, to about 30!

I continued to have an active social life. I played social tennis with my male friends. After burns, I found that my ground strokes were much the same, but my serves were lollipops due to my right shoulder constrictions.

For many years I had been playing tennis on Graham Brookman's tennis court with a group of friends. Then we moved to Michael Astley's court, but eventually wound up when I was about 80.

Soon after this Dr Mark Sheppard asked me to play with his group, which I gladly did until Mark turned 90 and was told not to play anymore.

Tess and I travelled widely including Europe, Africa, America and many Australian trips. Something I had felt I had not had time to do before.

R.G.M.H. and Family, on my 90th Birthday, Yalkuri Homestead, 2016.

Chapter 12

So, what happens now?

One day at the vegetable shop, I asked one of the very nice ladies serving, what she did with her spare time, and she said, "I am a trainer". To which I thought I was knowledgeable as I have teachers in the family, so I said, "What sort of teaching". She then laughed saying: "I am a personal trainer" (as in I help people get fit). I thought about this for a week and then asked her if she would be interested in helping me. She now comes for an hour, twice a week, and keeps me much fitter (I think).

I walk every day and on Wednesday mornings I go to the Prospect Council and volunteer my services (I like to call it work) as a Justice of the Peace. This I find interesting because I meet all sorts of different people with different nationalities, and they tell me lots of different stories. It can be everything from signing copies of documents to advice on power of attorney and medical attorney.

The highlight of Wednesday is after my 'work' I meet Alex and we have lunch at Muratti's with dessert fit for royalty.

I have for many years been playing bowls with the Adelaide Oval Bowling Club. We lost our rinks at the oval quite a few years ago and the Adelaide Bowling Club have kindly allowed us to play there.

I play a 'social' game on Tuesdays but this game of course is taken extremely seriously. Because of the damage to my hands and fingers, I find it difficult to not only hold but also to control the bowl. I do however manage, and together with Henry Krichauff we won the B grade double bowls competition a few years ago, and boy we were proud, and then for a second time this year (2018). The trophy proudly sits on my desk.

For me it is a good social outing and I must be one of the most senior (old) members of the club.

I enjoy gardening and maintaining my medium size garden, but I am not allowed up a ladder, so I enlist the services of Richard Mackie to help with the rest. I also have Irena who is a great help in the house, and with everything else.

I am extremely fortunate that I catch up with my children and Tess' daughter Rowie for dinner during the week. My 15 grandchildren pop in and see me and take me out for meals when they are in Adelaide and have a spare half an hour or so.

I am an avid supporter of the Australian String Quartet (ASQ) and attend as many performances as I can, and also enjoy the State opera.

So, life at 92 is good and miracles can happen.

A portrait by Rachel Smythe of Richard Harvey, 2006.

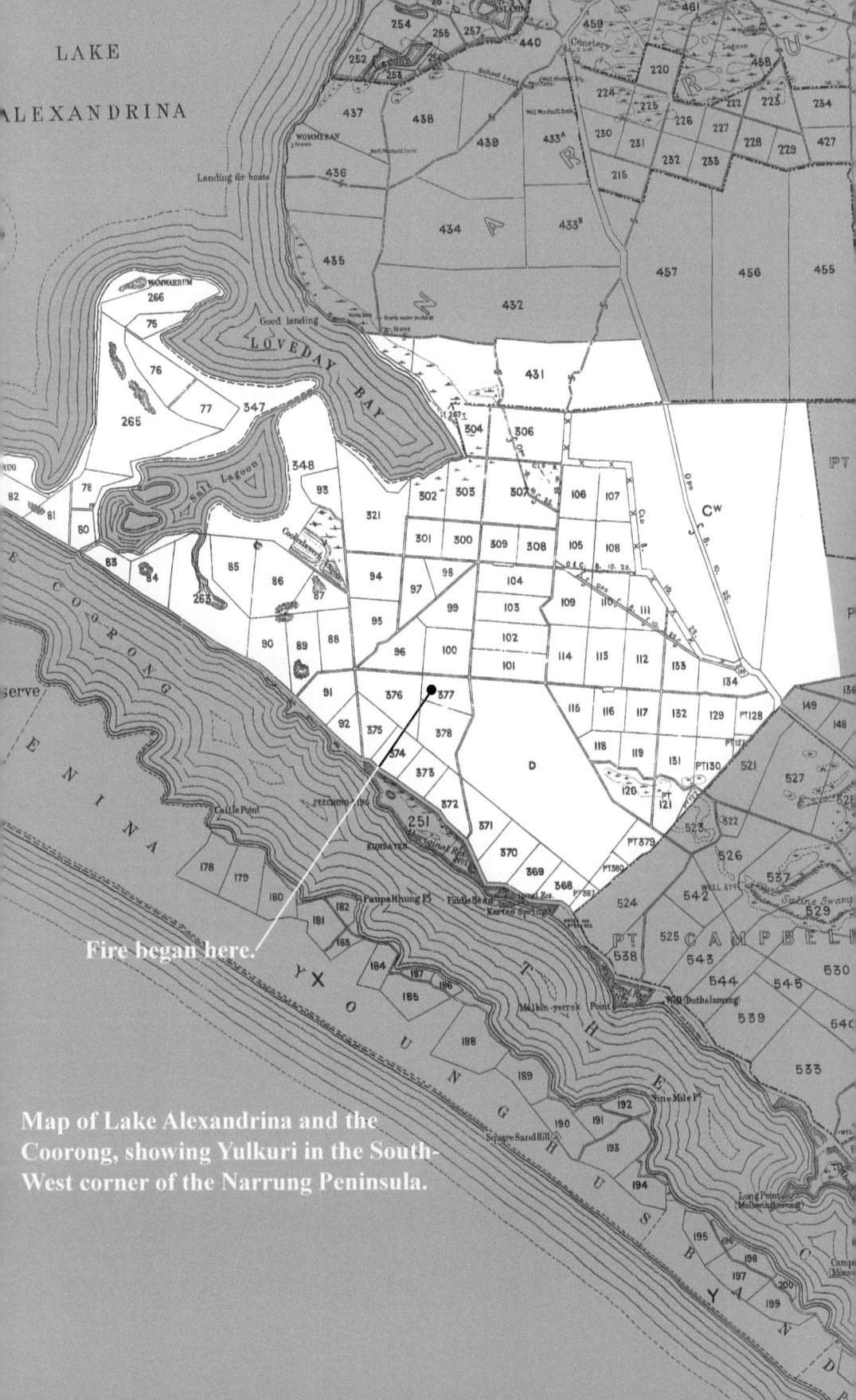

Map of Lake Alexandrina and the Coorong, showing Yulkuri in the South-West corner of the Narrung Peninsula.

www.ingramcontent.com/pod-product-compliance
Ingram Content Group UK Ltd.
Pitfield, Milton Keynes, MK11 3LW, UK
UKHW041903230426
12049UKWH00002B/30